THE CONQU *versus* EL

In 1070-71 Anglo-Saxons, Danes and armed monks entrenched on the Isle of Ely fought the final battle for the nation's liberty

TREVOR BEVIS

Based on the temporary booklet The Battle of Ely by the author

ISBN 0 901680 72 9

Published by Trevor Bevis BA, 28 St. Peter's Road, March, Cambs. PE15 9NA
Telephone: 01354 657286

Printed by David J. Richards, Printers & Stationers, 1 West Park Street, Chatteris, Cambs. PE16 6AH
Telephone: 01354 692947   Fax: 01354 692299

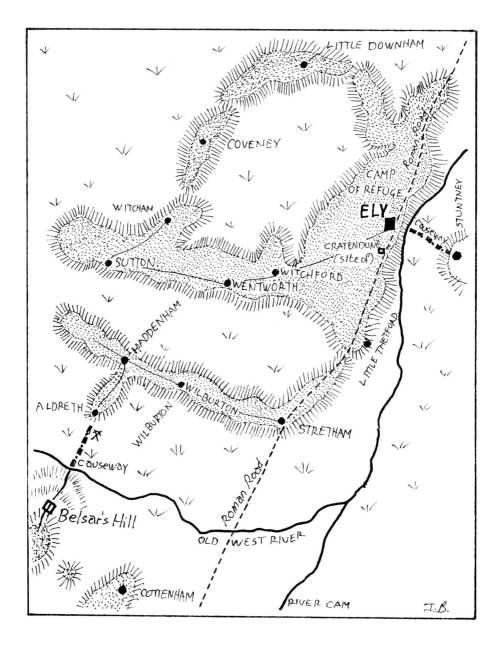

The Isle of Ely in 1070 showing sites of then existing causeways.
Belsar's Hill, a large historic earthwork, overlooks the Old West River crossed
by the King in his failed attempts to invade the Isle.

THE SCRIBES

Scholarly scribes took considerable care recording facts, testing rumours, even interviewing witnesses about events in English history. Monks attached to Ely and Peterborough monasteries were no exception to the rule.

An event of great importance took place in the Isle of Ely in the late 11th century. The King, buoyed up by his victory at Hastings in October 1066, quickly put down a number of uprisings in the country, but that occurring in the Fens was the most serious. Several documents by acknowledged chroniclers including Matthew Paris and William of Malmesbury refer to the trauma of Anglo-Saxons burdened by the yoke of Norman aggression. Their accounts covering the early years of Norman domination mention Hereward of Bourne who offered his mercenary skills to the beleaguered Anglo-Saxon force entrenched upon the Isle of Ely.

Writing in about 1150, Geoffrey Gaimer made a translation of *De Gestis Herwardi Saxonis* under the title *Lestorie des Engles*. This serves as proof that the first mentioned manuscript, the most comprehensive account of Hereward's embattled life and in particular his involvement with the defenders of the Isle of Ely, was written several years before Gaimer's translation. If De Gestis can be believed and the writer sees no reason why not, much of it is based on eye-witness accounts of men that had actually fought with Hereward The Outlaw, renowned mercenary and "leader of the soldiers."

Two reliable chroniclers, Hugh Candidus of Gildenburgh (Peterborough) and Robert of Ely, writing about their respective monasteries situated in the Fens, played significant roles investigating and collecting documentary evidence concerning what had been a prolonged and distinguished siege involving a number of "skirmishes" in the swamps and on higher ground. Hugh Candidus of whom it was recorded "wrote the truth" was no admirer of Hereward who ordered his Danish allies to seize and carry away a large amount of treasure from Peterborough abbey. Candidus wrote scathingly about the Dane's heavy-handed tactics.

De Gestis Herwardi Saxonis is mostly the work of Robert of Ely and his assistants. This is regarded as the authentic document pertaining to Hereward and, from a local point of view, a statement of what actually happened during the siege between the Norman army led by King William against the Anglo-Saxons and their Danish allies. By all accounts the siege was an epic one and captured the imagination of the English in succeeding centuries. Included in the Anglo-Saxon side were many of Hereward's mercenary friends who had accompanied him to foreign places and chose to fight with him on the Isle of Ely. They were recognised by the King himself as "men of valour." These same men were invited by monastic chroniclers to give account of Hereward and the famous siege.

Matthew Paris compiled the *"Chronica Majora"* in the 13th century and he mentions the Isle of Ely, one of the oldest land titles in the country. Concerning 1070-71 Paris states that many thousands of disaffected persons joined the resistance organised by Earls Morcar and Siward, supported by Aethelwine, Bishop of Durham. From this it is evident that spirited resistance commenced against William the First aided and abetted by the Anglo-Saxon Church. The insurrection in the north was dealt a severe blow by the Norman army and many Saxon participants looked to another region from whence to continue resistance. Geographically the Fens with its scattered islands offered the best choice, the marsh being a perfect barrier against besieging armies. From here resistance could be organised and maintained in reasonable security, the ultimate aim to arouse the Saxon nation to the cause of freedom. From the Isle resistance might be harnessed to a greater extent and eventually force the Normans away.

From 1066 to 1069 resistance operated from forests and wasteland, insurgents embarking on short, sharp attacks which did little more than hinder the Normans who, in turn, ransacked Anglo-Saxon communities and torched towns and villages, hanged the best workers and built castles in every shire. Rebels were relentlessly pursued but they had one more chance to achieve their aims and betook to the Isle of Ely, the dragon banner unfurled above the Fens. It was in the marsh around Ely that the remnants of the Anglo-Saxon army and its allies inflicted a great deal of damage to Norman might and pride. The Conqueror attempted to take the Isle by force and constructed causeways and bridges, but he reckoned without the wile and hardened experience of organised resistance and, through the combined efforts of the defenders and nature, lost hundreds of his best men.

Other accounts, too, add substance to the story so vividly captured by the imagination of authors like Charles Kingsley and William MacFarlane, who turned fact into romantic novels popularised by Victorians. Fuller wrote that when the siege had ended a Norman knight Basalius was stationed with thirty-nine armed colleagues at Ely monastery to subjugate a similar number of Benedictine monks. This statement is found in the *"Tabular Eliensis"* which commemorates the departure of the knights from Ely. Their stay was comparatively peaceful compared with the events at York and other places. Ely monastery was severely taxed by the Conqueror for its part in the siege. Stukeley made mention of ancient earthworks near Willingham "repaired by Norman soldiers" in preparedness for the siege of the Isle. The earthworks covering a large area is thought to date from Roman times or even before that period. This belief is substantiated in a manuscript *"A Story Found In The Isle of Ely"* (British Museum) in which it is stated that Belsar's Hill at Willingham overlooked a causeway above the marsh leading to Aldreth in the Isle.

These reports lead to very significant events taking place in the Fens approximately four years after the Battle of Hastings. The *Peterborough*

Chronicles compiled by Hugh Candidus, and more importantly *De Gestis Herwardi Saxonis* produced by Ely scribes supervised by master chronicler Robert, should be regarded as fitting testimonies to the Anglo-Saxons' final attempt to usurp the King. The insurrection not merely aggravated the Conqueror who, out of necessity, invested two-thirds of his army around the Fen perimeter; of far greater importance to his stoical opponents was their hope that such patriotic action would inspire a nation-wide uprising against him.

"I write of nothing and I speak of nothing save that which
I found recorded in the writings of old time, or
heard from the lips of faithful witnesses."

HUGH CANDIDUS - (The Peterborough Chronicles)

The Isle of Ely formed a natural fastness, perfectly protected by treacherous marsh and lakes. For hundreds of years it served the cause of rebellion, being fortified by barons, churchmen and royalty alike.

USE OF STRATAGEM

Four years after the Battle of Hastings won by the Norman invader in a single day, a protracted resistance began for possession of the Isle of Ely and its attendant villages occupying elevated ground in the middle of a vast watery wilderness. Ely and its environs dominated a malarial and hazardous background of near impassable marsh. The siege amounted to a war of guile against the Normans waged by professional Saxon and Danish soldiers aided and abetted by Anglo-Saxon nobility, the Church and remnants of the Anglo-Saxon fyrd from various parts of England. Ely's armed monks also engaged the enemy. This assembly of unusual allies on the Isle of Ely initiated a final resistance against the skill and determined might of the Norman army, arguably Europe's finest military machine. The resistance proved to be a contest of analytical skills between talented, hardened leaders, Hereward, a much-travelled and honoured mercenary of proved ability opposing the powerful, acquisitive and ambitious King William. Hereward and William the Conqueror were strategists of the highest order and battle proved.

Arising from the defeat by a narrow margin of King Harold, it is generally and incorrectly assumed that after that fateful event of 1066 William held all England in total subjection. In truth the Battle of Hastings, undeniably a milestone in the nation's progress, was the overture signalling the beginning of the end of the Anglo-Saxon epoch. However, it was not until at least four years later, in 1070-71, that the King could truly claim absolute authority over the English.

As befits an all-conquering army headed by an ambitious and efficient leader, sensible precautions become necessary in the wake of a successful initial conflict. A good military leader never puts his army at unreasonable risk. In the eleventh century most military victories were achieved on land. The right time and right place and correct deployment of cavalry and foot soldiers were every bit as important as the technical developments and advantages employed in modern warfare. In the eleventh century conquering armies had little advantage except valour and audacity in what was usually direct confrontation. This called for paramount skill in the use of spears, swords, arrows, javelins and the dreaded battle-axe. Military leaders developed the art of stratagem involving skilful use of ground and the ability to pre-assess the geological nature of potential battle sites. Battles were often close-fought affairs and victories not always the result of superior numbers. Much depended on awareness of deployment of opposed armies and known abilities and weaknesses of generals.

Inevitability of insurgent activities occupied King William's mind and his notorious flying columns progressed westwards and northwards carrying a clear message to the depressed population. It was a cruel business and some generals deemed it necessary to select a fit man from a settlement, the mainstay in husbandry skills who, having possibly displayed a form of resentment was seized and hanged from a tree. This barbaric sort of thing was done to instil into Saxon minds the futility of resistance and that it would be met by harsh measures.

On occasions armed Norman columns left villages engulfed in flames. In the early days of the King's progress through the land, hostility was fairly local, of a kind where perhaps a proud Saxon remonstrated with a Norman or demonstrated his hatred with obvious surliness or even threatened the man, actually attacking and killing him or injuring him. Such a thing would be met with death. William the Conqueror seized Saxon fortresses and old military earthworks, improving them with temporary timber fences and later erecting within the earthworks immensely strong stone walls and massive keeps. Some albeit in ruins, still remain. These formidable castles were designed to impress and subjugate Saxon peasants, and eventually these fortresses were enlarged to intimidate rebellious barons.

Through all the dangers and hustle and bustle of those formative years of Norman rule the King concentrated on law and order, acting ruthlessly when he considered it necessary. On only one occasion did he personally order the execution of an eminent Anglo-Saxon, Earl Waltheof, considered to be a skilled, potential instigator of insurrection. The earl was beheaded on the grounds of his unwelcome opinions. Later, the King appeared to relent of his action and by way of atonement allowed the body of the canonised Waltheof to be enshrined at Crowland abbey in the heart of the Fens.

To subjugate England's Saxon population proved difficult for the King. Uprisings occurred notably in the west and another was rapidly put down with horrific barbarity at York. The King's army reacted without mercy, hundreds of people receiving no quarter. By reason of logic the sacking of York ought to have clearly demonstrated to the Saxon nation the futility of resisting the armed might of the invading powers which, of course, was William's intention. For a time the Anglo-Saxon's kept a low profile but when opportunity allowed minor skirmishes still occurred. In hushed tones the Saxons talked over their hearths of woeful circumstances which had overtaken the nation.

The remaining vestige of power lay temporarily with Saxon abbots most of whom exercised office, some through the King's grace, holding onto their estates until they eventually retired or died, Norman churchmen then being appointed in their place. Several Norman abbots were in fact, militarists in their own right and commanded knights who accompanied them on their travels. The bitterness of defeat played upon Saxon minds for a long time, and after four years of Norman domination and consolidation of the new order it seemed that all hope of the emergence of a national saviour to lead the Anglo-Saxon race to freedom was lost forever.

LEADER OF THE SOLDIERS

A patriot was sorely needed to aspire for the nation's freedom. The King, busy asserting his authority in various parts of the land, was well aware that someone would challenge him and this spurred him to relentless action. Patriots were identified in several surviving Saxon earls but what was really needed was someone to co-ordinate resistance in a place convenient for an uprising but difficult for the aggressor. Hereward, so-called "The Wake" (in fact the son of Leofric of Bourne, grandson of Earl Radulf surnamed Scalre), proved to be the man, a skilled mercenary, a man of the Fens with foreign experience, possessor of vision and courage, a rebel at heart and a master tactician. Monastic accounts testify to Hereward as the scourge of foreign armies and honoured by foreign princes and kings who valued his assistance in routing their enemies.

According to *De Gestis Herwardi Saxonis* (The Adventures of Hereward the Saxon), as a youth he was irresponsible and "cruel in act," played severely and tended to deliberately stir up quarrels among those of his own age but, it was written, none were equal to himself in deeds of daring. He had a bad reputation and spared no person whom he knew to be a rival in courage or in fighting. Of his personal courage there is no doubt. His unseemly attitude led him to acts of sedition among the local population and he created tumult among the people living on his father's estate at Bourne. Unable to endure his son's escapades any longer and urged by the complaints of tenants, his father finally disowned Hereward and banned him from the area. He even implored King Edward to banish Hereward from the country and make known the harm he had committed against his parents and country. Thus Hereward became an outlaw, driven from his home and land in the eighteenth year of his age.

With Hereward gone, comparative harmony descended upon the local community and normality returned to his father's estate. Meanwhile, Hereward embarked on a dangerous course of adventures. Acknowledged as a master of military stratagem and able to size up situations and react quickly, he earned a famous reputation in foreign places. Well skilled in all forms of weaponry, and much sought after by foreign rulers, notably in Ireland and Friesland (parts of Holland), Hereward was eminently successful in battle and, according to ancient account was one of the most capable mercenaries of his time. While abroad, he married Turfrida, a member of a wealthy and eminent family.

Eventually Hereward learned of King Harold's death and subsequent invasion of England. Exercising utmost caution he returned home to discover his brother had been murdered and his late father's estate seized by a distinguished Norman. According to *De Gestis Herwardi Saxonis*, Hereward, greatly angered, with the help of some of his friends surprised the wrongful occupants when they were making merry and set about slaughtering them. Normans living in the vicinity were much alarmed at what had happened and left the estate alone. Hereward returned to the Continent and his exploits and valour went before him. However, England occupied his thoughts and he returned to the country, gathering around him friends and others of valour who under his expert leadership would form the backbone of Anglo-Saxon resistance in the Fens.

SAXON/DANISH ALLIANCE OPPOSED THE KING

As the King progressed from one rebellion to another, putting down insurrection, his agents informed him of developing problems in and around the Fens. Uprising in the West Country required his personal presence to assert total authority, only to be repeated on the banks of the River Dee and Mersey. Relentlessly the King brought the country to heel but one corner had not yet submitted. The Fens were rapidly becoming the Camp of Refuge.

For two hundred years Danish marauders sailing into the Wash estuaries were the scourge of Fen monasteries and towns, killing monks and nuns and setting fire to great churches. Accumulated treasures at these places attracted them. The last Danish incursion led by Osbeorn was actually favoured by the Isle inhabitants and others preparing resistance against the King. With backs to the wall the Saxons managed to negotiate a truce with Osbeorn and he agreed to assist the defenders in their defence of the Isle of Ely.

The Fens were uncommonly rich in ecclesiastical treasures at Ely, Peterborough, Ramsey, Thorney, Crowland, Spalding and a number of smaller religious houses scattered about the region. There were so many abbeys that the Saxons had long regarded the area as the Holy Land of the English and the inherited wealth had come to the ears of the King who intended to install Norman bishops, abbots and priors at these places. Peterborough was the more convenient monastery, the town rising onto the upland as well as having access to the Fens. The other monasteries and the Isle of Ely in particular were encompassed by malarial bogs, meres, water courses and those unfamiliar with the Fen were overwhelmed by seasonal obnoxious vapours.

Some Danes were already living on the fen islands and may have married local women. It is feasible that a few embraced the Christian faith. They admired a principled fighter and allied themselves to the cause of the rebels, recognising the proven abilities of Earls Tostig and Morcar. More especially did the Danes observe the unequalled leadership qualities of renowned mercenary Hereward whom the Earls, busily fortifying the Isle of Ely, had appointed leader of the soldiers.

Apart from telling of Hereward's experiences in foreign places *De Gestis Herwardi Saxonis* relates to his association with the Danes and well-known outlaws, also mercenaries, who had accompanied him to Friesland and other places. Hugh Candidus strongly berates Hereward's decision to attack Peterborough, the assault taking place in June 1070 but Hereward insisted that it was never his intention to destroy the town and monastery. The Danes made the journey in long-ships on the waterways and were opposed by monks who barred the monastery gates. It is not clear that Hereward accompanied the Danes but he certainly planned the assault in order to seize priceless artefacts from the church and carry them away to the Isle of Ely lest the newly appointed Norman abbot obtained them for his own use. The monks' unexpected opposition goaded the Danes into action and, according to the chronicler, they set fire to the gate and adjacent buildings, going about their task in a thorough Danish manner. The abbey church suffered no damage.

Leofric, Peterborough's Saxon abbot, was seriously wounded at the Battle of Hastings and returned to Peterborough broken in body and spirit. He died in November 1066. Thereafter the monks elected Brand, the provost, as their new abbot, this confirmed by Eadgar Aetheling, a scribe. Abbot Brand held the abbey for about three years and died at the time that King William was actively suppressing rebellions in the north of the country. The king appointed Turold, a severe man, as Abbot Brand's successor, and he was more familiar with military circles than cloisters. Peterborough's monks, mindful of the newly appointed abbot's attitudes, objected and besought Hereward's help to discourage the appointee who travelled from Stamford accompanied by several knights. The monks' attitude is understandable, Hereward none other than the nephew of Abbot Brand. Saxon monks had difficulty tolerating a Norman abbot. Hereward, too, was angered when he heard that a foreigner had been appointed to take charge of the abbey where, on a previous occasion, he received his knight's sword. The manner of bestowing a knighthood in Anglo-Saxon England was frowned upon by the Normans.

Eminent leaders sought sanctuary upon the Isle of Ely and their presence added to the insurgents' ranks. Aethelwine, Bishop of Durham, who had fled to Scotland undertook the hazardous journey to the Isle. Eadwine and Morkere took up arms against the king and the former was killed, but Morkere managed to reach the Isle and was joined by Siward, a distinguished Northumbrian. There is nothing conclusive in the suggestion that Stigand and Frithric of St. Albans fled to the Isle although some historians say they did. It is probable that armed men of the Fens joined the rebellion, and it is stated in *De Gestis Herwardi Saxonis* that "men from Berkshire" joined the cause. It is likely that men from other areas of the country came to the Isle and everything bade fair for a long campaign.

The Isle of Ely had been an embattled place for a long time. It seemed to be an excellent choice from which to resist invaders and the advantage was entirely with its defenders. Long ago an observer wrote: "The Fenland was of all parts of Britain, one of the best suited for the last remnants, either of a vanquished nation or of a vanquished political party to hold out against their enemy till the last. There is reason to believe that some isolated spots in this wild region had been held by remnants of the old Celtic inhabitants for ages after East Anglia and Mercia had become English ground. It is even possible that, here and there, an outlying British settlement may have lingered on to the days of William, and that Hereward, as well as Eadric on the other side of England, may have found allies among the descendants of those whom his father had displaced. In after days the land which had sheltered the last relics alike of British and English independence, sheltered the last relics of the party which had fought for the freedom of England by the side of Simon Montfort." (There is tangible proof indeed that the Celts influenced the Fen people. In the story of Thorney abbey, its three founders Tancred, Tortred and Tona practised the rules of Lindisfarne. Mr. Freeman cites a passage from the History of Ramsey Abbey as proof of the existence of Britons living in the Fens in the reign of Cnut. Thorney, it seems, marks the eastern extreme of Celtic influence in these parts, while at March a few miles away, Roman Catholic influence was established with the coming of St. Wendreda).

William the Conqueror's policy of erecting castles to intimidate local people included the Fen country which long before 1066 harboured a reputation of insurrection. He made his temporary headquarters at Cambridge castle, an earthwork and timber structure and prepared plans to blockade the Isle of Ely and starve the occupants into submission. The king built a turf castle at Wisbech overlooking the southern tip of the Wash, a strategic position commanding the Ouse estuary. His ships probably patrolled this expanse of water and guarded every inlet used by the Danes to carry men and supplies to Ely via the Fens' myriad of waterways. It says a great deal about the importance of developments in the Fens and of the king's concern as to what could happen if the insurgents remained unchallenged. As he later realised, they certainly would not be starved into submission and were entirely self-sufficient. Since they were surrounded with marsh he could not mount a direct assault from the upland, and he stationed a sizeable part of his army, two-thirds it is said, around the fen perimeter. Every approach road was covered and soldiers were stationed at temporary garrisons, as at Reach near Burwell where, according to *De Gestis Herwardi* the rebel army, including armed monks from Ely, skirmished with their Norman enemies.

The Saxon and Danish defenders were well equipped and very capable in the use of weapons. They were sustained from natural local resources and enjoyed a clear geological advantage over besieging Norman forces, being entirely familiar with hidden causeways in the marsh. As the siege lengthened, the Norman army became despondent, another advantage for the islanders who became more and more confident in their efforts to repel assaults. The king was well aware that the insurrection was becoming a serious hindrance to his plans and might easily spill into the upland regions initiating a general rebellion throughout the country. That is what the Saxon earls and Hereward hoped would happen. Here in the Fens chances

William The Conqueror's army approached the Isle on a narrow causeway of timber and inflated hides. It was repulsed by Anglo-Saxon defenders.

Water and marsh at Aldreth reminiscent of that encompassing the causeway 979 years ago. According to chroniclers the Conqueror lost hundreds of men in his failed attempts to take the Isle by force.

of success were better than had been the case in other areas of the country. Defenders had ample time to prepare barricades and took advantage of the strategic platform surrounding by marsh seemingly impassable to besieging armies. The Isle of Ely was a natural fastness from which were launched swift, murderous forays against Norman outposts and against the uplands.

"Now the men in the Isle of Ely had begun to hold the island against King William who had taken England in war. Hearing of the return of Hereward they sent for him with all his men to take part with them in the defence of the country and the liberty of their fathers . . . These messages were delivered to Hereward more especially in the name of Thurston, abbot of the Church at Ely, the Isle being their domain and it were they that had rendered it defensible against the King, more particularly because he designed to set a foreign monk over them, one of those monks for whom he had already sent from the French nation to appoint as deans and heads in all the English churches." - *(DE GESTIS HERWARDI SAXONIS)*

HUNDREDS PERISHED

Initially the King planned to attack the Isle from an easterly direction, making use of water linked to the Ouse near Brandon. This point is indicated by Reach Lode an ancient waterway forming a confluence with the River Cam. The Norman army was repulsed with heavy loss of life, said to be hundreds, on the water courses and in the marsh. Such loss of life was unacceptable and the King abandoned all thought of taking the Isle from that particular direction. He considered using the Roman road between Cambridge and Ely, but this was subjected to flooding from the River Ouse and therefore not much better.

Thereupon the King turned his attention to a site further west and had equipment moved to a ridge of land bordering Smythie Fen. There, the fen formed part of a narrow strip of water and marsh between the upland and southern shores of the Isle of Ely at a place known as Aldreth. It was written that Hereward, attired as a workman, joined labourers working for the King and he observed everything William was doing. The King caused a vast amount of material to be moved to a large site opposite the Old West River known as Belsar's Hills, believed to a Roman earthwork although some think it is much older. The material, stones, trees, animal hides and hemp were conveyed to the spot by a fleet of boats. Everything was transferred to the encampment adjacent to the village of Willingham. Bentham wrote: *"The camp occupied by the Conqueror's army when he besieged the Isle of Ely is still visible at the south end of Aldrey (Aldreth) Causeway, within the manor of Willingham and is corruptly called Belsar's Hills."*

Reference to the site is made in De Gestis Herwardi Saxonis: *"Abrehede ubi minus aquis et proecinqitur insular"* The Ely History (Liber secundus, 229) compiled by monks, states *"Alrehethe, ubi aquae insular minus latae sunt."*

This refers to an island or promontory jutting into a lake or marsh. On the strength of the manuscript kept at the British Museum, Belsar's Hills derives its name from Belasyus, the Norman general in charge of operations.

From advantageous heights of the Isle, the Saxon defenders could see the Norman army and labourers constructing the causeway. Each day it drew nearer to the camp of refuge. The Saxons and their allies made determined efforts to interrupt the work, and it was written that in this vicinity Hereward achieved his greatest success against the Norman army. According to *De Gestis* his organised forays against the Conqueror's workmen and soldiers were "sudden, mysterious and murderous."

"When the King heard of these things (alluding to the strengthening position of insurgents on the Isle of Ely) he was excessively angry . . . First he moved his army to Alrehede which was not so wholly surrounded with water and swamp . . . After bringing instruments and engines on logs and stones and piles of all sorts, they constructed a causeway in the swamp, though it was comparatively useless and narrow, near to the great river flowing through the place. They also put into the water very large trees and beams bound together and beneath them sheepskins tied together, turned after flaying and inflated with air, so that the weight of a man going over it might be better borne. - (DE GESTIS HERWARDI SAXONIS)

This early example of a bailey bridge proved to be unsuccessful. Apart from being too narrow and unstable the artificial causeway had not only to cross the swamp deep enough to drown men especially when burdened with heavy armour, it also had to penetrate the thick screen of sedge which grew up to fourteen feet high and gave defenders ideal cover.

A hail of arrows rained upon the Norman army from defenders well hidden in the sedge and on the land. The causeway being narrow there was no room to manoeuvre and in their panic to escape the missiles large numbers of men fell into the swamp and were dragged down with the weight of chain mail. The Norman army suffered heavy losses and the few survivors had no choice than to return along the ill-fated causeway to comparative safety of their base at Willingham.

"When the causeway had been completed, a great multitude of men rushed upon it, eager among other things to get to the gold and silver which was thought to be plentifully hidden on the Isle, with the result that those men who, in their haste had taken the lead, were drowned. The causeway, being unstable, collapsed into the marsh with the men upon it. They that were in the middle of the assailing company were also swallowed up in the deep swamp. Few indeed of those who followed last abandoned their arms and with difficulty managed to escape, tumbling out of the water and through the sand. Although hardly a man pursued them, they perished in great numbers in the water and in the swamp; and of those that perished, up to this day are drawn from the depths of those waters in rotten armour. – (DE GESTIS HERWARDI SAXONIS)

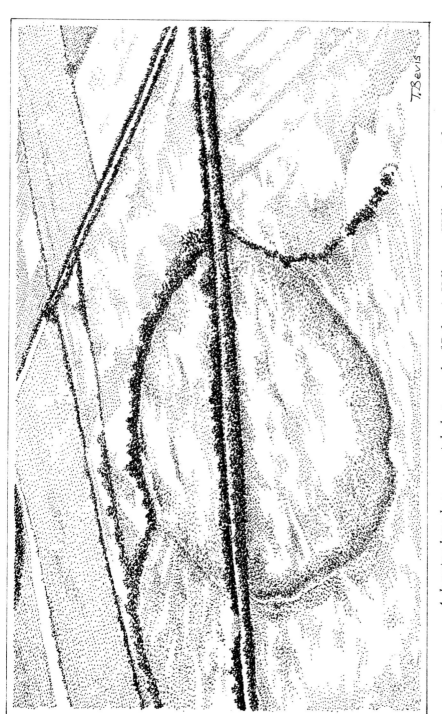

A drawing based on an aerial photograph of Belsar's Hill, near Willingham, said to have been used by the King as a base camp for men and supplies in his disastrous attempts to subjugate the Isle of Ely. The track through it links with Aldreth Causeway where it is said hundreds of Norman soldiers lost their lives.

De Gestis states that Hereward, who seems to have been a master in the art of disguise, infiltrated the Norman camp at Brandon where the King set up temporary headquarters. Hereward's guise evidently failed him on one occasion when a young servant boy, suspicions aroused, sounded the alarm, but the Saxon patriot managed to escape. The manuscript might be regarded as an early biography of the Fen hero and tells of his Royal opponent's desperation to find a way into the Isle and the rebellion be put down. Despite his failure to cross the marsh on rafts held up by inflated skins, the King was persuaded by certain generals to repair it and try again. This time, however, with the help of a witch carried forward in a wheeled tower towards the Isle, followed by a large number of knights and foot soldiers. Reluctantly the King authorised the attempt. While the witch hurled forth incantations at the Saxon defenders, they in turn allowed the soldiers to approach within a few yards of the shore, then fired burning arrows into the water, setting fire to oil which the defenders had previously poured onto the marsh. The conflagration engulfed the witch and many Norman soldiers perished in that fatal attempt to subjugate the Isle. Their comrades withdrew and from a safe distance watched the marsh as it turned into a sea of flames destroying all trapped within it. The King turned on his advisers and berated them, declaring that never again would he undertake such a foolish action.

Yet one Norman did actually set foot on the Isle and was taken prisoner. Highly impressed with the gallantry and nobility of its defenders, the man was escorted around the place and allowed to observe the enemy about their business.

"Of all those mentioned . . . not one got into the Isle, except by mere chance a single, eminent knight called Dada, who was at the very front. No man defending the Isle was caught in the snare, for some had made a heap of sods on the bank of the river (West Water) in front of the bulwark's ramparts, laying ambushes on the right and on the left. The King observing these things from a distance, saw how his men at the front of the column were swallowed up by the swamp and drowned in the water. Groaning with heartfelt sorrow with those of his men who had survived – very few compared with the dead – the King departed, laying aside all hope of making any further attack against the Isle. Instead, he placed stockades here and there with soldiers round about, lest the Saxon islanders should have free access to lay waste the district beyond the marsh.." - *(DE GESTIS HERWARDI SAXONIS)*

We will learn more of the extraordinary experiences of Dada, the Norman knight, on another page.

One of the stockades erected by the King was that at Belsar's Hill. This guarded the narrow entrance from the Isle into the upland area near Willingham. A temporary fortress was also set up at Reach, near Burwell where, according to De Gestis, at least one skirmish took place between Saxons and the Norman garrison. A Norman soldier observed that some rebels were, in fact, armed monks that had volunteered to take an active part in the action. It was a source of amazement and unbelieveable that monks ventured to take up the sword. Never before had the Norman soldiers experienced anything like it. Ely's monks were determined that a foreign priest should not rule at Ely, but their courage was to no avail.

William the Conqueror's problems arising in various parts of the country paled in comparison with the dangerous task confronting them on the Isle. Strategic know-how had served them well in the west and in the north of the country and Anglo-Saxon resistance quickly melted away. The Ely experience was much more prolonged than the King had bargained for and the Isle proved a tough nut to crack. The battle of Hastings was over in a few hours. Even so, for William and his army it was a near thing. At least a year would elapse before the King would stand before the grey bulk of Ely monastery and only then could he say that the whole of England was his at last.

Upon the Isle stout Saxon hearts mustered for the final showdown and standards fluttered bravely from elevated ground overlooking the squalid, vaporous marsh below. The forces of nature favoured them, raised bulwarks invested with water all around. The scene was daunting to the King and try as he might he was unable to penetrate the morass in safety. William did not relish the clash of steel with an enemy of known doggedness and who certainly enjoyed every advantage of fighting in the marsh. In the end the Anglo-Saxons and their allies were not subdued by straight-forward military expertise, and most through treachery, were obliged to go into hiding.

The Camp of Refuge held out for many months, but the King reckoned even though the marsh be against him, time would be on his side and the shortage of essentials and threat of seizure of monastic lands would achieve for him what force of arms could not do. Having suffered heavy loss of men he was unwilling to deplete his army by unreasonable methods. He made it known to Ely's monks that if they continued to help the rebels they would suffer great privation. They ought to demonstrate their powers to the insurgents and oblige them to leave then make a secret rendezvous with him. The abbot, fearful of losing all his possessions, caused the Norman army to be shown a secret way into the Isle. Elements of resistance were quickly overcome but several of Hereward's lieutenants fled and fought another day. Historians surmise that many of the Isle's courageous defenders fell to the sword, but nobody knows for certain and ancient manuscripts do not mention a contest to the bitter end.

Earl Morkere threw himself at the mercy of the King and his reward was imprisonment for life at a castle in Normandy where there was less risk of him influencing Saxon dignitaries. Siward the thane met a similar fate. Hereward, warned by a monk that enemy soldiers had gained access to the Isle threatened revenge. His immediate reaction was to set fire to the abbey, but persuaded by his informer not to do so, the leader of the soldiers left the Isle. *De Gestis* tells us that he sought refuge in the "Wide Sea" and adapted to the role of a guerrilla with them. He observed the soundness of defence works and was impressed by the bearing and skill of the soldiers many of whom were mighty men. Then for a second time he was taken before important dignitaries and questioned.

The knight placed in order of importance the three earls, Adwinus, Morkere and Tosti and there were two nobles, Orgar and Thrachitell nicknamed The Boy. Dada gave a glowing account of Hereward The Outlaw and his men. He told the King that all of them were accomplished soldiers and were above themselves and above all knights he had ever seen in France or in the Roman Empire or in Constantinople for valour and courage. Some may equal Hereward, he said, but none could surpass him.

These remarks angered the Duke of Warenne, himself an eminent knight, whose brother had seized Hereward's father's estate at Bourne and was slain by the aggrieved son. He accused Dada of allowing himself to be deceived and of trying to induce the King to show kindness to his enemies. It was, the Duke said, false and specious praise and he was indignant that Hereward, an enemy, be upheld by Dada in the matter of valour. In reply, Dada insisted he had not been bribed to say these things, nor was any favour promised in the future, except as a prisoner he had sworn on oath to speak only the truth.

The King commanded that Dada should be regarded as harmless for what he had seen and spoken of, and he extolled him to tell more, reminding the council he had long known Dada to be a truthful man. Dada submitted himself to a period of questioning by the King and others. They asked him whether the Isle's defenders suffered any shortage of provisions and if there were more famous men in addition to those he had already named. This was to see if he contradicted himself. More important, that the court might learn something to help them uproot their soundly entrenched enemies.

Dada told the assembly that the Anglo-Saxons were furious at the King for appointing monks from across the sea to head English churches. The appointments irritated the abbot and monks of Ely who could not tolerate the idea of having a foreigner set above them. They preferred to protect their domain by working to survive rather than be reduced to slavery. The abbot and monks encouraged outlaws and nobles to gather at Ely. Famous individuals that had gathered on the Isle to defend the Church and surrounding Fens were not only famous but were also condemned and disinherited people. Many were young and even their parents came with them. Everyone worked diligently to fortify the Isle of Ely against the King.

SPEARS AND SHIELDS HUNG IN READINESS

"Within the Isle," said Dada, "the defenders lived with little or no pressure upon them, this by reason of the size of their army. Although the Isle is blockaded, nothing seems to affect daily existence. Ploughmen regularly go about their tasks and the reapers' hands do not waver in harvest time, nor does the hunter neglect his hunting spears and the fowler constantly lies in wait for birds by the banks of the rivers and in the woods.

"The inhabitants are abundantly supplied with all kinds of living creatures. For at this time the waterfowl change their feathers and appearance. I saw several men bring many little birds, sometimes a hundred, occasionally two hundred and even more, and very often not many less than a thousand from one single piece of water. From the woods of the Isle of Ely, in the same way, at one time in the year there is a great supply of herons, to say nothing of the abundance of wild animals and cattle. Then again, the waters around the Isle abound with every kind of fish. Need I say more? Every day that I spent on the Isle, living in the English manner, I felt disgust at seeing the banquets in the monks' refectory. Soldiers and monks sat together for dinner and supper. The abbot with the three Earls already named, and two distinguished men, namely Hereward and Turkillas surnamed Pure, seated side by side.

"Above each knight and monk shields and lances hung against the walls, and in the middle of the hall from one end to the other were breastplates and helmets and other pieces of armour. All these were conveniently positioned so that the soldiers and monks were quickly ready to take their turn and embark on warlike expeditions. In all truth, this one thing above all others struck me as marvellous. Of all the things I noticed, the monks of Ely are remarkably well adapted to warfare. It is something I have never heard of before and I have never experienced such a thing in any other place. It seems the people of the Isle are not deficient in anything pertaining to their defence, except perhaps in personal courage, while they have such a fertile place beyond doubt most productive in every kind of seed and grain. It is so well protected by water and swamp. All this gives it more strength than any castle surrounded by walls. Yet I trust my lord the King will not cease to struggle against them. My account is quite truthful and it may be better to make peace with them than get nowhere at all."

BURWELL ATTACKED BY ELY MONKS

When Dada had finished speaking, a soldier who had been ordered by the King to direct the construction of a blockade near a dyke at Reach, spoke in support of him. "The things Dada speaks of are quite credible. Only yesterday I saw men coming from the Isle, not a large number, about seven, wearing soldiers attire and carrying weapons. Without any doubt all but two were monks. They were well acquainted with warfare like the soldiers on the Isle, and they claimed to exercise the rights of a soldier. The monks started fires at Burwell and inflicted mischief in every direction, running all over the place.

"Some of our men, ten in number, working up front on the blockade, without thought to their own safety hurried towards the Isle men hoping to capture them. They came up against them at the dyke within distance of throwing lances. There was a lot of fighting and all but one of our men died. He managed to escape. Our man, Richard, a fine soldier, grandson of the Viscount Osbertus was hotly pursued by a man called Wenochus.

"While the fight between these two waged on watched by the rest of the Isle men, their leader, Hereward, caused the combatants to separate and forbade anyone to offer violence to Richard. He said it was unworthy for two or three to assault one and that on no account would he allow such a thing. This we learned from Richard himself. We followed the Isle men to their ships and killed one of the soldiers with a javelin and caught another."

The Norman soldier then told the King the names of the raiding party, namely Hereward the leader, Wenochus, Turstanaus – a young man surnamed Warder - Boter of St. Edmunds, Siwardus, Levricus and Acer the Hard so-called for his ability to endure. Although most of them were monks they were very distinguished and approved in military knowledge. Led by Hereward they often made trial of valorous deeds.

The King listened intently to all this and said nothing, obviously in his way crediting his enemies as men of valour and that it was unworthy to regard them in a lesser light. Yet he could not extol his enemies in front of his own army. He contemplated the possibility of making peace with them as he well knew the Isle of Ely was not only protected by exceedingly brave men but they had also the forces of nature on their side. It seemed an impossible task to prevent the Isle defenders from leaving their camp and returning to it again.

KING WANTED PEACE WITH THE ISLE MEN

Summoning his nobles and counsellors, the King explained what was in his mind. That he proposed to make peace with the Isle men. It was, he said, too serious a thing to leave such men in the rear of activities when the army ought to be marching against the Danes and, after that, to go directly to Normandy. Some of the elders present and those closest to him began to dissuade him from such reasoning. They told the King they had not forgotten that the insurgents had invaded their estates (seized from the original Anglo-Saxon owners) and had taken shares of their rightful possessions.

The King was left in no doubt as to his counsellors' attitudes. He was told, "If you dismiss the insurgents without punishment, the same who have long and vigorously opposed your rule will regard you as being weak and the rebels will have no need to beg for freedom humbly and with prayers. Any rights you grant to them will declare a weakness on your part. All men will mock your superiority and will not be afraid to act likewise in your dominion." (It was due to the King's harsh actions that previous uprisings in the country were ruthlessly and effectively put down).

The King angrily replied that, as things stood, he could not take the Isle of Ely or any other place so naturally fortified by the power of God. One of his knights, Ivo Taillebois, suggested that victory could be achieved if the King considered a possible alternative and employ a sorceress whom he himself personally knew, that she might use her skills to crush all resistance on the Isle. This was approved by the Court and the King yielded to the idea that the proposed action be attempted, and ordered that the old woman be brought to him. Then he assembled his army in strength and surrounded the Isle, guarding all approaches, and ordered a causeway to be constructed across the swamp with the hired witch at the forefront of operations.

Hereward, however, knew all this in advance and prepared to ambush the soldiers as they approached the shores of the Isle. As already stated, oil was poured onto the water and set alight. The Saxons, hidden behind earthworks and rough briars poured arrows onto the causeway and soldiers crossing it, causing great carnage.

An eyewitness wrote: " . . . Extending two furlongs the fire, rushing hither and thither among them formed a horrible spectacle in the marsh, and the roar of the flames with the crackling twigs and brushwood and willows made a terrible noise. Greatly alarmed, the Norman soldiers tried to flee, each man for himself . . . Very many were suddenly swallowed up (the causeway collapsing beneath stampeding feet) and others drowned in the same waters and were overwhelmed with arrows. For in the fire their javelins were no good against groups of men emerging cautiously and secretly from the Isle to repel them. Among them, that woman of infamous art, hysterical with fear, fell down head-first from her lofty frame and broke her neck."

The King himself, attired for war, marched with his men and was among those that managed to escape from the flames. He carried in his shield on his way to the camp at the rear, an arrow that had struck deep. All around, his men loudly bewailed the loss of friends. The King calmed them and said he had no wound to complain of but, said he, "I do complain that I did not take a sound design from all those submitted to me. That is why so many of our men have fallen, deceived by the subtlety of an infamous woman and moved without knowledge of her detestable art, even to listen to whom ought to have been for us an accursed thing. But for this these things would not have happened to us."

So it was left to the Church to betray the last great Anglo-Saxon army assembled on its fastness, the Isle of Ely, the final battle ground between Norman and Saxon armies. The scribe recorded: "This was done on a certain day that it might not come to Hereward's knowledge. The abbot's messengers were graciously received by the King and he with his army by means of a secret way hastened to the Isle of Ely. Alwinus, one of Ely's monks, found Hereward and warned him that the King had made a covenant with the King. Thus ended the siege of a year's duration.

NOTES;

IT IS WRITTEN Hereward "took refuge on the Isle of Ely." He did in fact volunteer to return to England to observe his father's estate at Bourne, held by a Norman magnate. Hereward later involved himself with events taking place on the Isle of Ely where he became chief soldier opposing the Conqueror. A "Camp of Refuge" was formed on the Isle of Ely and the Anglo-Saxons chose the place for their final stand. They hoped that the Isle would become a springboard for insurgents to ferment a national uprising against the invader. The famous siege is mentioned in several manuscripts written by scribes in the 13th century.

DE GESTIS HERWARDI SAXONIS can be regarded as the biography of Hereward the patriotic Saxon. While some myth may pertain to certain events, much of content relating to eyewitness accounts can be regarded in a factual light. Earl Morcar, one of the prominent participants in the siege, held 2½ carucates of land at Bourne *(Domesday Book)* and would certainly be familiar with the family of Hereward.

HEREWARD held land from the Abbot of Crowland: "They say that St. Guthlac's land which Ogler holds in Rippingale was the monks' demesne farm, and that abbot Ulfkil (of Crowland) granted it to Hereweard at farm, as might be agreed between them each year. But the abbot took possession of it again before Hereweard fled the country because he had not kept the agreement." *(Domesday Book)*. (Hereward returned to the Continent but he later came back with his followers and joined Earls Morcar and Tosti on the Isle of Ely).

WILLIAM DE WARENNE , founder of several castles and priories and a member of the King's retinue, questioned the monarch's admiring attitude towards the Isle garrison. Another person could have been thrown into prison for such audacity. Warenne married the Conqueror's daughter and probably felt he had licence to contradict the King.

HEREWARD had descended from a family of Earls of Mercia, his father described as Leofric of Bourne, grandson of Earl Radulf surnamed Scalre. Apparently Earl Leofric had no link with the Wake family. The Wake's are an old Northamtonshire family and somehow, probably through marriage with a descendant of Hereward, the surname Scalre was assigned Wake. The Wake's deemed it an honour to include Hereward, a famous man, with their family name.

THIS BOOKLET is based on a previous temporary publication *"The Battle Of Ely"* by the author. His other publication *"Hereward Of The Fens"* incorporates the complete *"De Gestis Herwardi Saxonis"* (in English) relating to the life and adventures of Hereward.

THE CONQUEROR
versus ELY

A problem with deep history is the tendency for myth to over-ride fact. This little book attempts to lift recorded facts to an acceptably believable level and explains what happened in the Fens more than 900 years ago. It was the time when a new nation was being forged; when Anglo-Saxon and Norman blood began altering the course of English history and founding a new destiny for the nation. One that affected the world in many ways and conceived the greatest empire ever known.

The Battle of Hastings in 1066 was over in less than a day and, by all accounts, was a close-run thing. For the following five years the Conqueror was hard pressed putting down uprisings in the land, these carried out expeditiously and ruthlessly, the Saxons aspiring to encourage a nation-wide rebellion and hopefully eject the invader from the land. The rebellion on the Isle of Ely is mentioned in various 13th century manuscripts.

The Anglo-Saxons' hope was best realised on the Isle where, led by Hereward, nobles and eminent Churchmen held out against the King for a year until the abbot of Ely, weary of events, arranged for him to enter the Isle by a secret route. Thus ended the Saxons' epic resistance seriously envisaged by the King as potentially threatening his rule.

~~~~~~

ISBN 0 901680 72 9   **£2.40**